Smelling

in Living Things

Karen Hartley, Chris Macro, and Philip Taylor

Heinemann Library
Chicago, Illinois

©2000 Reed Educational & Professional Publishing
Published by Heinemann Library,
an imprint of Reed Educational & Professional Publishing,
Chicago, IL
Customer Service 888-454-2279

Designed by Celia Floyd
Illustrated by Alan Fraser
Originated by Ambassador Litho
Printed in Hong Kong / China

06 05
10 9 8 7 6 5 4
Library of Congress Cataloging-in-Publication Data
Hartley, Karen, 1949-
    Smelling in living things / Karen Hartley, Chris Macro, and Philip
Taylor.
        p. cm.
    Includes bibliographical references and index.
    Summary: Describes how the sense of smell works in humans and
animals and how they use it.
    ISBN 1-57572-249-6 (lib. bdg.)
    1. Smell Juvenile literature. 2. Nose Juvenile literature.
[1. Smell. 2. Nose. 3. Senses and sensation.] I. Macro, Chris,
1940- . II. Taylor, Philip, 1949- . III. Title. IV. Series:
Hartley, Karen, 1949-   Senses.
QP458.H34 2000
573.8'77—dc21   99-38259
                                                        CIP

Acknowledgments

The Publishers would like to thank the following for permission to reproduce photographs:-

Ardea London/Ian Beames, p. 21; Bruce Coleman/Andrew Purcell, p. 29; Bruce Coleman/Hans Reinhard, p. 22; Bruce Coleman/Jane Burton, p. 28; Heinemann/Gareth Boden, pp. 4,.5, 6, 7, 8, 10, 12, 13, 14, 15, 24, 25, 26, 27; Image Bank/Paul McCormick, p. 18; Oxford Scientific Films/Frederick Ehrenstrom, p. 17; Pictor International, p. 20; Richard Greenhill, p. 11; Tony Stone/Daniel J. Cox, pp. 16, 23; Tony Stone/Kevin Summers, p. 19.

Cover photograph reproduced with permission of Oxford Scientific Films and Gareth Boden.

Every effort has been made to contact copyright holders of any material reproduced in this book. Any omissions will be rectified in subsequent printings if notice is given to the Publisher.

Some words are shown in bold, **like this**. You can find out what they mean by looking in the glossary.

CONTENTS

WHAT ARE YOUR SENSES?

Senses tell people and animals about the world around them. You use your senses to feel, see, hear, taste, and smell. Your senses make you feel good and warn you of danger.

Senses are important to you and other animals. This book is about the sense of smell. You will find out how the sense of smell works and what you use it for.

WHAT DO YOU USE TO SMELL?

You smell with your nose. That is the only place you can sense smells. Noses can be different shapes and sizes, but they all work the same way.

Your nose has two small **nostrils** that are close to your mouth. The nostrils have many small hairs inside. The hairs keep you from breathing in dust and **grit.**

nostril

HOW DOES A NOSE WORK?

The smell of an orange is made of very tiny pieces of the orange. The pieces are too small to see or touch. They mix with the air you breathe and go up your nose.

The tiny pieces touch smell **receptors** inside your head. The receptors give your brain a message. Then your brain tells you what you are smelling.

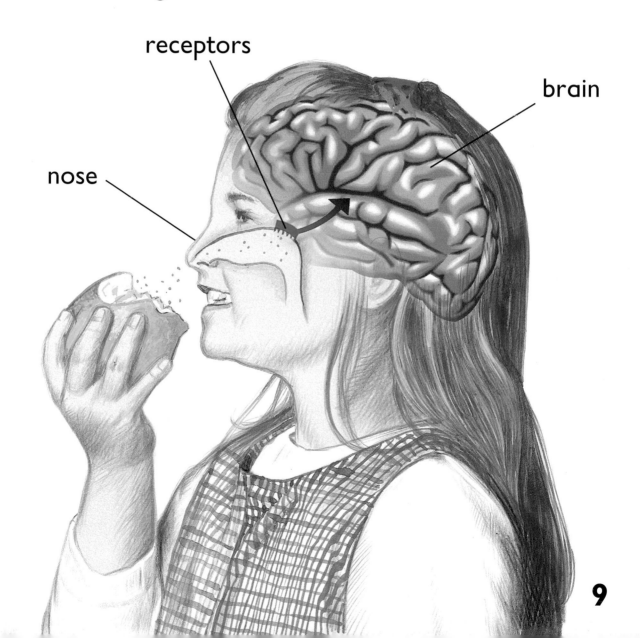

receptors

brain

nose

HOW DOES YOUR NOSE HELP YOU?

Your sense of smell helps you feel hungry when you need to eat. When you smell food, your mouth makes **saliva** to get ready for the meal.

Some smells are from things that are bad for you. When you smell them, you can move away from them. Some smells, such as smoke from a fire, warn you of danger.

USING YOUR NOSE

Your sense of smell tells you that food is cooking and is nearly ready. Smell can also tell you if the food has cooked too long.

Your sense of smell helps you taste things. The smell of food in your nose makes the food taste good. The smell makes you want to eat it.

WHAT CAN HAPPEN?

If you have a cough, cold, or **sinus** trouble, your nose can get blocked. You cannot breathe easily, and you lose the sense of smell for a while.

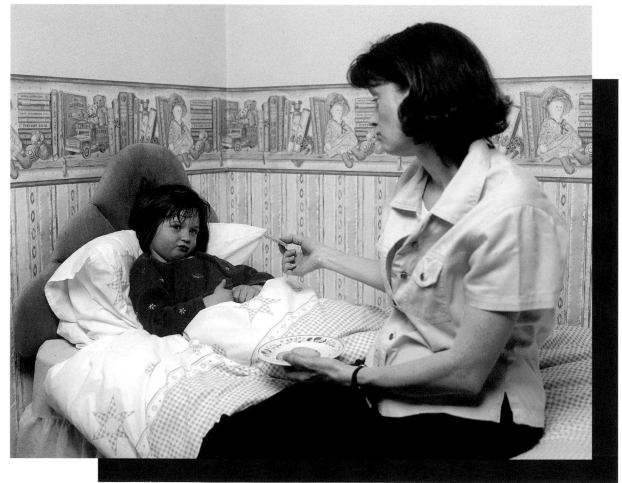

There are many cough drops, tablets, nose drops, and other **medicines** that can help clear your nose. When you can breathe easily and smell things again, you feel better.

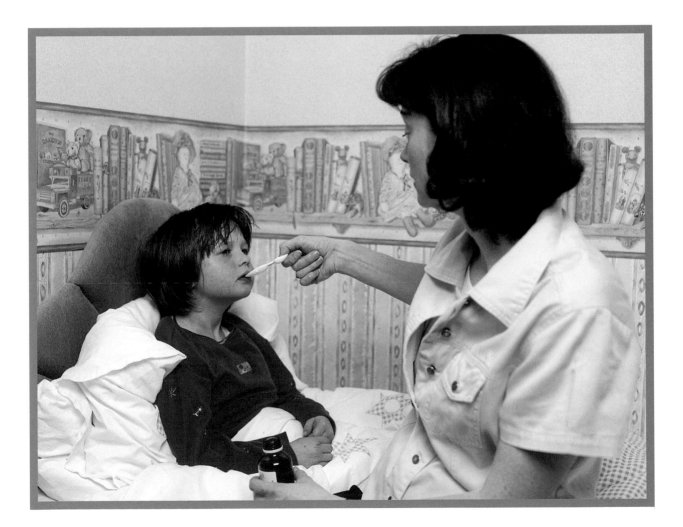

DO ANIMALS HAVE NOSES?

Most animals have some way of sensing smells. Monkeys and apes have noses very much like you. Their noses work the same way as yours.

Many fish have **nostrils** at the front of their head. They can smell **scents** when water flows over a special pouch as they swim.

OTHER WAYS TO SENSE SMELLS

Insects, such as bees, have **antennae** with smell **receptors** at the ends. Some flowers have strong **scents**. Bees' antennae sense the smell and guide them to the flowers.

Snails have two pairs of antennae. They stretch the short ones out in front as they move. They use the antennae to smell what is around them.

HOW DO ANIMALS USE SMELLS?

Animals use their sense of smell to find food. Smell tells them when they are home. Smell helps them know who the other animals are.

Ants have **antennae** that they use to smell strangers in their **colonies.** Only ants that smell like them are allowed into the nest.

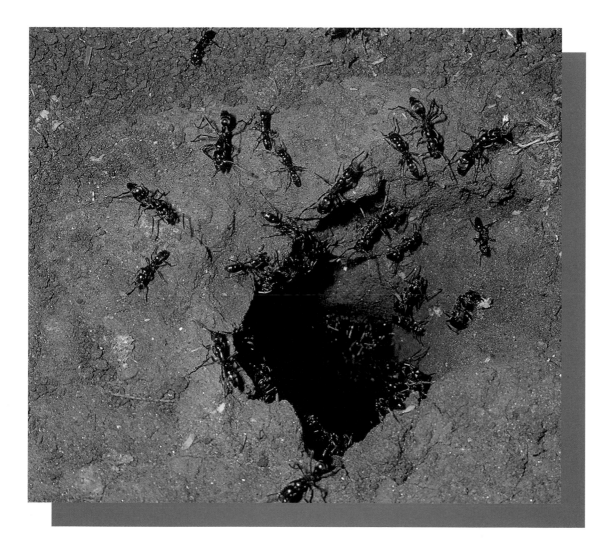

USING SMELL TO STAY SAFE

Deer have a very good sense of smell. They can sniff the wind to smell danger. They can smell animals that could be hunting them. Deer run away quickly to escape.

A skunk can make a very unpleasant smell when it is alarmed or in danger. This **odor** can stop its enemy from following it.

INVESTIGATING WITH YOUR NOSE

How good is your sense of smell? Some flowers have stronger **scents** than others. Can you name different types of flowers just by the scent they make?

Ask someone to put different food into jars and cover the jars with cloth. Do not look inside. Can you name the food just by sniffing?

PLAYING TRICKS ON YOUR NOSE

If you cannot smell, it is hard to taste the difference between foods. Hold your nose while someone puts a piece of raw onion on your tongue. Then do the same with a piece of raw carrot. Can you taste a difference?

Sometimes smells remind you of places you have been. The smell of shells and seaweed can remind you of a vacation at the seashore.

DID YOU KNOW?

Some fish have an amazing sense of smell. Trout like to eat shrimp. They can smell the **scent** of shrimp even when the shrimp are far away.

Moths have long **antennae** that they use for smelling. Some male moths have a strong sense of smell. They know when a female moth is nearby or even miles away.

GLOSSARY

antenna (more than one are called antennae) long, thin growth that helps some animals know what is around them

colony name for a group of insects that live together

grit tiny piece of stone or sand

medicine special drug used to treat or cure illness

nerve something that carries messages from the body to the brain

nostril opening in the nose that lets air in

odor a smell, also called a scent

receptor cell in the body that can sense what is around it

saliva water that is made in the mouth to keep the mouth wet and help digest food.

scent a smell, also called an odor

sinus space in the bones of the head that is connected with the nose

SENSE MAP

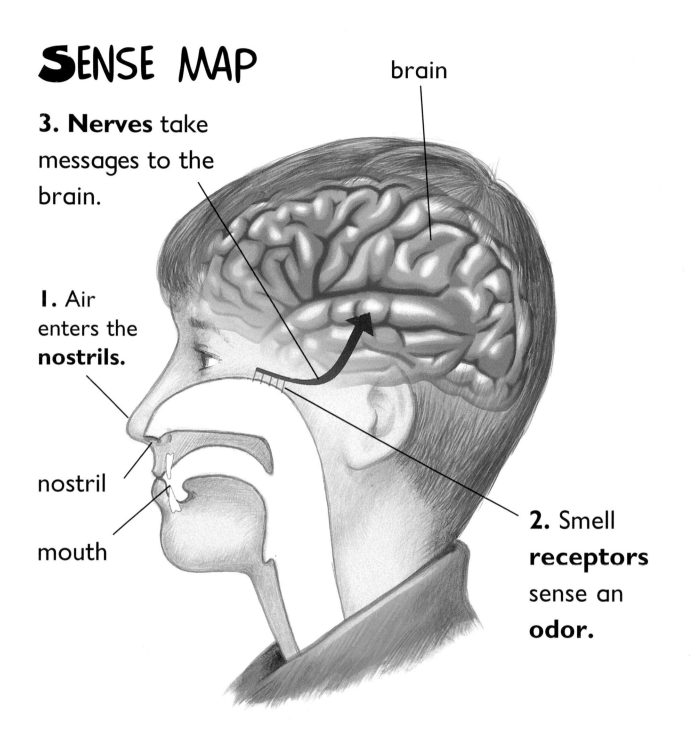

brain

3. Nerves take messages to the brain.

1. Air enters the **nostrils.**

nostril

mouth

2. Smell **receptors** sense an **odor.**

MORE BOOKS TO READ

Ballard, Carole. *How Do We Taste and Smell?* Austin, Tex.: Raintree Steck-Vaughn, 1998.

Pluckrose, Henry. *Sniffing and Smelling.* Austin, Tex.: Raintree Steck-Vaughn, 1998.

Pringle, Laurence. *Smell.* Tarrytown, N.Y.: Marshall Cavendish, 1999.

INDEX